Elegant Assets

The Insider's Guide to Investing in Luxury Handbags

Table of Contents

Introduction

Chapter 1:

    The Allure of Luxury Handbags

Chapter 2:

    Understanding the Handbag Market

Chapter 3:

    Icons of Luxury - History and Noteworthy Bags of Top Brands

Chapter 4:

    Evaluating Investment-Worthy Handbags

Chapter 5:

    Authenticity and Quality

Chapter 6:

    Buying and Selling Designer Handbags

Chapter 7:

    Risks and Rewards of Handbag Investing

Chapter 8:

    Care and Maintenance of Investment Handbags

Chapter 9:

    The Future of Handbag Investing

Conclusion

Appendices

    Glossary of terms.

    Directory of resources for authentication, buying, and selling.

    Reference list of key handbag models from top brands.

Introduction

Welcome to a journey that intertwines the elegance of high fashion with the acumen of investment strategy. This book is dedicated to unraveling the complexities and delights of investing in designer handbags, a realm where artistry meets appreciation and luxury intersects with profitability.

The Allure and Value of Luxury Handbags as Investment Pieces

Luxury handbags are not merely accessories; they are embodiments of history, craftsmanship, and exclusivity. Beyond their immediate aesthetic and functional appeal, these pieces hold a unique place in the investment world. Unlike many assets, a well-chosen designer handbag can maintain or even increase in value over time. The reasons are manifold: the prestige of the brand, limited production runs, enduring designs, and the often-fascinating stories behind iconic models. This book explores the multifaceted nature of handbags as investment pieces, delving into why and how they transcend their role as fashion items to become valuable assets.

Purpose and Structure of the Book
This book aims to guide both newcomers and seasoned collectors through the

Chapter 6:

    Buying and Selling Designer Handbags

Chapter 7:

    Risks and Rewards of Handbag Investing

Chapter 8:

    Care and Maintenance of Investment Handbags

Chapter 9:

    The Future of Handbag Investing

Conclusion

Appendices

    Glossary of terms.

    Directory of resources for authentication, buying, and selling.

    Reference list of key handbag models from top brands.

nuanced world of investing in designer handbags. Whether you are a fashion enthusiast keen to understand the investment potential of your passion, or an investor looking to diversify your portfolio with non-traditional assets, this guide is crafted for you.

- **Structure of the Book**:
    1. **Understanding the Market**: We begin by exploring the landscape of the luxury handbag market, its history, and its current dynamics.
    2. **Key Players**: Delving into the stories of top luxury brands, understanding their iconic

models, and what makes them sought after in the investment world.

3. **Investment Strategies**: Covering how to assess potential investment pieces, understanding authenticity, and the importance of condition and provenance.

4. **Navigating Buying and Selling**: Insights into the buying process, maintaining and storing your investments, and strategies for selling.

5. **The Future of Handbag Investing**: Looking ahead at

emerging trends and how they might shape the market.

Our journey will equip you with the knowledge to make informed decisions, understand market trends, and appreciate the artistry behind these exquisite pieces. As you turn each page, you'll gain insights that will help you navigate the fascinating world of designer handbags, not just as symbols of style, but as valuable assets.

emerging trends and how they might shape the market.

Our journey will equip you with the knowledge to make informed decisions, understand market trends, and appreciate the artistry behind these exquisite pieces. As you turn each page, you'll gain insights that will help you navigate the fascinating world of designer handbags, not just as symbols of style, but as valuable assets.

Chapter 1

The Allure of Luxury Handbags

Defining Luxury in the Context of Handbags

The term 'luxury' in the context of handbags transcends mere material wealth or brand status. It encapsulates a realm where craftsmanship, exclusivity, design, and history converge to create objects that are much more than mere accessories. Understanding luxury in handbags involves several key dimensions:

1. **Exceptional Craftsmanship**
   - **Artisanal Skill**: Luxury handbags are often the product of exceptional

artisanal skill and meticulous attention to detail. They are crafted using time-honored techniques, often passed down through generations.

- **Quality of Materials**: These bags are made from the highest quality materials, whether it's the finest leather, exotic skins, or unique fabrics. The selection of materials plays a crucial role in the bag's aesthetic, durability, and feel.

2. **Exclusivity and Rarity**

- **Limited Production**: Luxury handbags are frequently produced in limited quantities, adding to their exclusivity. Some are even made to order or released as limited edition collections, making them rare and highly sought-after.

- **Unique Designs**: Many luxury handbags are the result of unique, creative designs that set them apart from mass-produced items. They often reflect the artistic vision of renowned designers and can be considered works of art in their own right.

3. **Brand Heritage and Status**
    - **Historical Legacy**: Luxury brands often have a rich heritage, with stories that add depth and character to their handbags. This history, which may include decades or even centuries of

fashion evolution, contributes significantly to the brand's status and the perceived value of its products.

- **Symbolism**: Owning a luxury handbag is not just about functionality or aesthetics; it's also a symbol of personal style, status, and an appreciation for the finer things in life. For many, these handbags signify a certain attainment and are a form of self-expression.

4. **Investment Value**

- **Appreciating Asset**: Unlike many consumer goods, luxury handbags from certain high-end brands can appreciate in value over time. This

released as limited edition collections, making them rare and highly sought-after.

- **Unique Designs**: Many luxury handbags are the result of unique, creative designs that set them apart from mass-produced items. They often reflect the artistic vision of renowned designers and can be considered works of art in their own right.

3. **Brand Heritage and Status**
    - **Historical Legacy**: Luxury brands often have a rich heritage, with stories that add depth and character to their handbags. This history, which may include decades or even centuries of

fashion evolution, contributes significantly to the brand's status and the perceived value of its products.

- **Symbolism**: Owning a luxury handbag is not just about functionality or aesthetics; it's also a symbol of personal style, status, and an appreciation for the finer things in life. For many, these handbags signify a certain attainment and are a form of self-expression.

4. **Investment Value**
    - **Appreciating Asset**: Unlike many consumer goods, luxury handbags from certain high-end brands can appreciate in value over time. This

makes them not just a purchase for personal enjoyment but also a potential investment.
- **Resale Market**: There is a vibrant secondary market for luxury handbags, where collectors and fashion enthusiasts seek out vintage, rare, or limited-edition pieces, often willing to pay a premium for them.

In essence, luxury in the context of handbags is a multi-faceted concept that goes beyond just a high price tag. It represents a synthesis of artistry, exclusivity, heritage, and an enduring appeal. These handbags are treasured not only for their tangible qualities but also for the intangible joy and prestige they bring to their owners.

The Emotional and Aesthetic Appeal of Designer Handbags

Emotional Connection

- **Symbol of Personal Achievement**: For many, acquiring a designer handbag is a symbol of personal success or a milestone. It can represent the fruition of hard work and aspirations, making the bag much more than just an accessory.
-

- **Sentimental Value**: Designer handbags often carry sentimental value, especially if they are gifts, heirlooms, or reminders of special occasions. This emotional connection can elevate a handbag from a mere object to a cherished possession.
- **Expression of Identity**: Handbags are extensions of personal style and identity. They can be reflections of one's taste, personality, or even mood. For many, choosing a handbag is a deeply personal decision tied to how they want to present themselves to the world.

Aesthetic Appeal

- **Beauty and Design**: Designer handbags are celebrated for their beauty and exquisite design. From sleek, minimalist lines to ornate, decorative details, these bags are visual delights that appeal to those with a keen eye for style and artistry.
- **Trendsetting Pieces**: Often, designer handbags are at the forefront of fashion trends. Owning a trendsetting bag can be thrilling for fashion enthusiasts, as it allows them to be part of the ever-evolving world of high fashion.

- **Quality of Craftsmanship**: The aesthetic appeal of designer handbags is also in their craftsmanship. The feel of luxurious leather, the precision of the stitching, and the perfection of the finish contribute to their overall beauty.

The allure of designer handbags lies in a blend of emotional resonance and aesthetic beauty. They are not just functional items but symbols of personal journeys, fashion statements, and artworks. This combination of emotional and aesthetic appeal makes designer handbags much more than just accessories; they are integral parts of personal expression and style.

Historical Significance and Modern Relevance of Designer Handbags

Historical Significance

- **Cultural Reflections**: Throughout history, handbags have not just been accessories; they've reflected social changes, cultural movements, and fashion evolutions. From the practical designs of the early 20th century to the statement pieces of the modern era, handbags have mirrored the changing roles and attitudes in society, particularly regarding women's independence and style.

- **Artisan Heritage**: Designer handbags have a rich heritage of craftsmanship. They embody traditional techniques and skills passed down through generations, showcasing the art of leatherworking, metalworking, and textile creation. This historical artisanship is a testament to the dedication and creativity of the craftsmen and serves as a connection to the past.
- **Fashion Icons and Trends**: Over the decades, certain handbags have become iconic, often associated with prominent figures or fashion eras. It became a favorite of celebrities and royalty, symbolizing a blend of luxury

and practicality. These iconic bags not only hold a place in fashion history but also continue to influence contemporary designs.

Modern Relevance

- **Evolving Designs and Materials**: Today's designer handbags are at the intersection of traditional craftsmanship and modern innovation. Designers experiment with new materials, shapes, and technology, ensuring that handbags remain relevant and desirable in the ever-changing fashion landscape.
- **Luxury and Status Symbols**: In contemporary society, designer

handbags are more than functional items; they are symbols of status, taste, and personal identity. They are often seen as investments in one's image and style, reflecting an individual's position and lifestyle.

- **Sustainability and Ethical Fashion**: There is a growing emphasis on sustainability and ethical practices in fashion. Luxury brands are increasingly adopting eco-friendly materials and responsible manufacturing processes, making designer handbags relevant to a new generation of environmentally conscious consumers.

The allure of designer handbags lies in their rich history and their ability to stay relevant in modern times. They are not just fashion accessories but cultural artifacts that tell stories of craftsmanship, societal change, and personal expression. As we continue to witness the evolution of fashion, designer handbags remain at the forefront, continually adapting, and reflecting the times while holding onto their storied pasts.

Chapter 2

Understanding the Handbag Market

The Economics of the Luxury Handbag Market

The luxury handbag market is a significant sector within the broader fashion industry, characterized by its unique economic dynamics. Understanding these dynamics requires examining several key aspects:

1. **Market Value and Growth**
   - **High-Value Industry**: The luxury handbag market represents a multi-billion dollar industry globally. It has shown consistent growth over the years, driven by rising affluence, global

consumer demand, and an increasing appreciation for luxury goods.

- **Market Resilience**: This market has demonstrated remarkable resilience in the face of economic fluctuations. Even during downturns, luxury handbags have maintained or increased their value, underlining their appeal as alternative investments.

2. **Price Dynamics**
   - **Premium Pricing**: Luxury handbags command high prices due to their quality, brand reputation, and exclusivity. The pricing often reflects the cost of materials, craftsmanship,

and the brand's marketing and retail expenses.

- **Value Appreciation**: Certain handbags from prestigious brands have the potential to appreciate in value over time. Limited editions, collaborations, and classic models from brands like Hermès, Chanel, and Louis Vuitton are particularly known for their investment potential.

3. **Consumer Behavior and Demand**
   - **Brand Loyalty and Aspiration**: Consumers of luxury handbags often exhibit strong brand loyalty, influenced by the brand's heritage, exclusivity, and status symbol. The

aspirational quality of luxury brands plays a significant role in driving demand.

- **Emerging Markets Influence**: The growth of emerging markets, particularly in Asia, has significantly contributed to the expansion of the luxury handbag market. Increasing wealth and a growing middle class in these regions have led to higher consumption of luxury goods.

4. **Supply Chain and Production Costs**
- **Controlled Supply**: Many luxury brands maintain exclusivity by controlling supply. Limited production runs and selective distribution

channels ensure that the supply of certain handbag models remains lower than demand, contributing to their exclusive status.

- **Production and Sourcing Costs**: The cost of sourcing high-quality materials and employing skilled artisans contributes to the high prices of luxury handbags. Many luxury brands also invest heavily in maintaining traditional craftsmanship methods.

5. **Secondary Market and Resale Value**
- **Robust Resale Market**: There is a thriving secondary market for luxury handbags. Platforms like The RealReal, Vestiaire Collective, and auction

houses have made it easier for consumers to buy and sell pre-owned luxury handbags.

- **Vintage and Rare Handbags**: Vintage handbags and rare limited editions often fetch high prices in the resale market, often exceeding their original retail prices.

The economics of the luxury handbag market is characterized by high-value transactions, strong brand-driven demand, and significant investment potential. This market not only reflects the financial aspects of luxury goods but also encompasses cultural and emotional dimensions, making it a unique and complex sector within the world of fashion and investments.

Market Trends, Consumer Behavior, and Driving Factors in the Luxury Handbag Market

Understanding the luxury handbag market requires an in-depth look at the current trends, consumer behavior, and the factors driving these dynamics. This market is influenced by a variety of elements, from global economic conditions to evolving fashion sensibilities.

Market Trends

- **Sustainability and Ethical Fashion**: There's a growing trend towards sustainability in the luxury market. Consumers are increasingly aware of the environmental and ethical implications of their purchases, leading brands to focus on sustainable practices and materials.
- **Digital Influence and Online Shopping**: The rise of e-commerce has significantly impacted the luxury handbag market. Brands are investing in online platforms and digital marketing strategies to reach a broader audience. Social media also

plays a crucial role in shaping trends and influencing consumer choices.

- **Resurgence of Vintage and Classic Styles**: Vintage and classic handbags from renowned brands are experiencing a resurgence in popularity. This trend is partly driven by nostalgia and a preference for timeless designs that hold their value.

Consumer Behavior

- **Brand Loyalty and Aspiration**: Luxury handbag consumers often exhibit strong brand loyalty, influenced by the heritage and exclusivity associated with certain brands. There is also an aspirational aspect to luxury.

handbags, with consumers viewing them as symbols of status and success.

- **Emotional Purchases**: Buying a luxury handbag is frequently an emotional decision, driven by the desire for self-reward, expression of personal style, or as a celebration of milestones.
- **Global Demographics**: The luxury handbag market is seeing a shift in its consumer base. Younger generations, including Millennials and Gen Z, are becoming significant consumers in the luxury market, bringing different preferences and shopping habits.

Driving Factors

- **Global Economic Conditions**: The state of the global economy plays a critical role in the luxury handbag market. Economic prosperity generally leads to increased consumer spending on luxury goods, while downturns can affect purchasing behavior.
- **Innovations in Design and Technology**: Advancements in design and technology are important driving factors. Innovations in materials, manufacturing processes, and design techniques contribute to the creation of new, desirable handbag styles.
- **Cultural and Celebrity Influences**: Cultural trends and celebrity

endorsements have a significant impact on the luxury handbag market. A single endorsement or appearance with a particular handbag can instantly boost its popularity and demand.

The luxury handbag market is a dynamic arena, shaped by a complex interplay of trends, consumer behavior, and various driving factors. From the impact of digital technology to the growing emphasis on sustainability and the ever-changing preferences of global consumers, understanding these elements is key to grasping the nuances of this vibrant market.

- **Expanded Markets**: Globalization has opened new markets for luxury handbags, particularly in emerging economies like China, India, and the Middle East. The rising wealth in these regions has created new demographics of luxury consumers.
- **Cultural Exchange**: The cross-cultural exchange facilitated by globalization has led to a fusion of styles and preferences, influencing handbag designs and trends. Luxury brands often incorporate diverse cultural elements into their collections to appeal to a global audience.

- **Supply Chain Dynamics**: The global nature of supply chains has allowed luxury brands to source materials from around the world, often seeking the best quality and craftsmanship. However, it also brings challenges related to logistics, sustainability, and ethical sourcing.

Impact of Digitalization

- **E-Commerce Growth**: Digitalization has significantly boosted e-commerce in the luxury handbag market. Brands have embraced online retailing, either through their own platforms or through luxury e-commerce sites, making luxury handbags more accessible to a broader audience.

- **Digital Marketing and Social Media**: The rise of digital marketing and social media has dramatically changed how luxury brands engage with consumers. Instagram, Facebook, and other platforms are now crucial for marketing, brand storytelling, and customer engagement.

- **Market Data and Consumer Insights**: Digital tools and analytics provide brands with valuable data on consumer behavior, preferences, and trends. This data drives decision-making, from design to marketing and retail strategies.

- **Counterfeit and Authentication Challenges**: Digitalization has also made it easier for counterfeit products to be produced and distributed, posing a challenge for luxury brands. As a response, many brands are investing in advanced authentication technologies and digital tracking systems.

Globalization and digitalization have had a profound and multifaceted impact on the luxury handbag market. They have expanded the reach and scale of luxury brands, created new opportunities for engagement and sales, and introduced complexities related to cultural adaptation, supply chain management, and online authenticity. As these trends continue to evolve, they will shape the future landscape of the luxury handbag market, presenting both challenges and opportunities for brands and consumers alike.

Chapter 3

Icons of Luxury - History and Noteworthy Bags of Top Brands

History of Chanel: The Brand and Their Handbags

The Founding of Chanel

- **Early Beginnings**: Chanel was founded in 1910 by Gabrielle "Coco" Chanel, opening her first shop at 31 Rue Cambon in Paris, initially focusing on hats. Coco Chanel's vision was to redefine feminine fashion with a focus on simplicity and elegance, a stark contrast to the elaborate styles of the time.

- **Expansion into Couture**: In 1915, Chanel expanded into couture, and by the 1920s, the brand had become a symbol of sophisticated, understated fashion. Chanel introduced the concept of the "Little Black Dress," revolutionizing women's evening wear.

Emergence of Chanel Handbags

- **The Introduction of Chanel 2.55**: In February 1955, Coco Chanel introduced the Chanel 2.55 handbag, a design that would become an enduring icon. The bag featured a quilted leather design and a chain
-

- shoulder strap, a departure from the typical handbag styles of the time.
- **The Chanel 2.55's Design Innovations**: The 2.55 was practical yet elegant, designed with Chanel's ethos of liberating women from cumbersome fashion. The bag's shoulder strap allowed for hands-free use, a feature inspired by Chanel's desire for functionality in women's fashion.
- **The Mademoiselle Lock**: The original 2.55 featured a rectangular turn-lock closure, which Coco Chanel referred to as the "Mademoiselle Lock," referencing her never-married status.

The Evolution of Chanel Handbags

- **Karl Lagerfeld's Influence**: In the 1980s, Karl Lagerfeld, the brand's creative director, reintroduced the 2.55 with some modifications, including the now-iconic CC lock. Lagerfeld played a crucial role in reviving and maintaining the brand's relevance in modern fashion.
- **Variations and Collections**: Over the years, Chanel has introduced various iterations of the 2.55, including different sizes, colors, and materials, ensuring the design remains both classic and contemporary.
- **The Boy Chanel**: In 2011, Chanel launched the Boy Chanel, a handbag

line inspired by a cartridge bag designed for hunters. It was named after Coco Chanel's great love, Boy Capel, and represented a mix of masculine and feminine style elements.

Chanel Today

- **Continued Legacy and Innovation**: Chanel continues to be a leading name in luxury fashion, constantly innovating while maintaining its heritage. The brand's handbags remain a symbol of luxury and high fashion.
- **Investment Pieces**: Chanel handbags, particularly the classic models, are

considered investment pieces. They are known for retaining or increasing in value, making them sought after not only by fashion enthusiasts but also by collectors and investors.

The story of Chanel and its handbags is one of innovation, elegance, and timeless appeal. From Coco Chanel's revolutionary designs to Karl Lagerfeld's modern interpretations, the brand has continuously evolved while staying true to its original ethos of simplicity, functionality, and refined elegance. Chanel's handbags, more than just accessories, are emblematic of the brand's enduring legacy in the world of fashion.

History of Louis Vuitton: The Brand, Handbags, and Luggage

Founding and Early Years

- **Establishment**: Louis Vuitton was founded in 1854 by Louis Vuitton Malletier in Paris. Initially, Vuitton's focus was on creating high-quality, durable travel trunks.
- **Innovative Trunk Design**: Louis Vuitton revolutionized luggage design by introducing flat-topped trunks made of Trianon canvas, a departure from the traditional dome-topped

trunks. This design was more stackable and practical for travel.

Expansion and Innovation

- **Customization and Popularity**: The brand quickly gained popularity, and Vuitton began customizing trunks for high-profile clients. This bespoke service established the brand as a symbol of luxury and exclusivity.
- **Introduction of the Monogram Canvas**: In 1896, Louis Vuitton's son, Georges Vuitton, created the iconic LV Monogram Canvas. This design was an effort to prevent counterfeiting, one of the earliest instances of a fashion brand fighting piracy.

Growth in the 20th Century

- **Expanding Product Range**: Throughout the early 20th century, Louis Vuitton expanded its product range beyond trunks to include smaller travel items like bags and accessories.
- **The Keepall Bag**: In 1930, Louis Vuitton introduced the Keepall bag, a softer, more portable version of the traditional luggage, marking the brand's foray into handbags.
- **The Speedy Bag**: The Speedy bag, introduced in the 1930s, became one of Louis Vuitton's most popular

handbags, initially made for Audrey Hepburn in a smaller size.

Post-War Expansion and Diversification

- **Global Expansion**: After World War II, Louis Vuitton expanded internationally, opening its first store in the United States.
- **Diversification**: The brand diversified its product range, introducing new handbag designs, wallets, and other leather goods.

Modern Era and Continued Legacy

- **Creative Directors**: Marc Jacobs joined as the creative director in 1997, introducing Louis Vuitton's first ready-to-wear clothing line. Nicolas Ghesquière later took over, furthering the brand's fashion influence.

- **Iconic Collaborations**: Louis Vuitton has collaborated with various artists and designers, blending luxury with art and fashion, including partnerships with Stephen Sprouse, Takashi Murakami, and Supreme.
- **Innovation in Luxury Handbags**: Louis Vuitton has continued to innovate in the realm of luxury handbags, introducing new designs while maintaining the quality and style that the brand is known for.

Legacy and Influence

- **Symbol of Luxury**: Louis Vuitton remains a symbol of luxury, known for its quality craftsmanship, iconic designs, and the distinctive Monogram Canvas.
- **Cultural Impact and Recognition**: The brand has become deeply embedded in cultural fashion discourse, recognized globally for its contributions to luxury fashion and luggage.

The history of Louis Vuitton is a story of innovation, expansion, and the pursuit of luxury. From its beginnings as a maker of quality travel trunks to its status as a global fashion powerhouse, Louis Vuitton's journey is a testament to its enduring commitment to craftsmanship, design excellence, and luxury.

Gucci: A Legacy of Innovation and Luxury in Fashion and Handbags

The Founding of Gucci

- **Early Beginnings**: Gucci was founded in 1921 in Florence, Italy, by Guccio Gucci. Initially, the brand specialized in leather goods and was inspired by the luxury luggage that Guccio saw while working in hotels in Paris and London.
- **Influence of Equestrian World**: The brand's early designs were heavily influenced by equestrian gear, reflected in its now-iconic symbols

such as the horsebit and the green-red-green web.

Expansion and Iconic Styles

- **Post-War Expansion**: After World War II, due to material shortages, Gucci innovatively used canvas for its products, introducing the diamond pattern that became synonymous with the brand.
- **Rise in Popularity**: In the 1950s and 1960s, Gucci gained international fame. Hollywood stars and jetsetters were frequently seen with Gucci bags, making them a symbol of luxury and sophistication.

The Gucci Handbag: A Symbol of Luxury

- **The Bamboo Bag**: One of Gucci's most famous handbags, the Bamboo Bag, was introduced in 1947. Its bamboo handle, created out of necessity during wartime rationing, became an iconic design element.
- **Jackie Bag**: Named after Jacqueline Kennedy, the Jackie Bag became popular in the 1960s and remains a timeless piece of Gucci's handbag collection.
- **Dionysus and Other Modern Designs**: Gucci has continually reinvented its approach to handbag design with items like the Dionysus bag, blending modernity with its rich heritage.

Creative Renaissance and Modern Era

- **Tom Ford Era**: In the 1990s, under the creative direction of Tom Ford, Gucci underwent a transformation, introducing a more modern, sensual aesthetic that reinvigorated the brand.
- **Alessandro Michele's Vision**: Since 2015, under Alessandro Michele, Gucci has embraced a maximalist, eclectic style that has garnered a new generation of fans. Michele's approach has successfully fused historical references with contemporary design, redefining luxury fashion.

Gucci's Legacy and Cultural Impact

- **Fashion Innovator**: Gucci has consistently been at the forefront of fashion innovation, blending its rich Italian heritage with contemporary trends.
- **Symbol of Status and Style**: Gucci handbags have become more than luxury items; they are symbols of status and style, often seen as investments in personal style and fashion history.
- **Sustainability and Social Responsibility**: In recent years, Gucci has moved towards sustainability and social responsibility, recognizing the

importance of these values in modern luxury fashion.

The history and legacy of Gucci in the world of luxury handbags highlight a journey of innovation, craftsmanship, and a keen understanding of fashion's evolving landscape. From its equestrian-inspired beginnings to its status as a staple of modern luxury, Gucci's handbags embody the fusion of timeless elegance with cutting-edge design, securing the brand's place in the pantheon of fashion giants.

Christian Dior: Elegance and Innovation in Luxury Fashion and Handbags

Founding and Early Impact

- **Establishment**: Christian Dior was founded in 1946 by the eponymous designer in Paris, France. The brand revolutionized women's fashion post-World War II.
- **The New Look**: In 1947, Dior introduced the "New Look," featuring cinched waists, voluminous skirts, and a feminine silhouette. This radically different style redefined women's

fashion and instantly gained acclaim, re-establishing Paris as the center of the fashion world.

Expansion and Brand Evolution

- **Diversification**: Following the success of its couture collections, Dior expanded into perfumes, with the launch of its first fragrance, Miss Dior, in 1947. The brand eventually ventured into accessories, makeup, and skincare.
- **Global Influence**: Christian Dior quickly became a symbol of French luxury and elegance, gaining popularity among Hollywood stars and international elites.

Christian Dior Handbags: A Symbol of Luxury

- **Introduction of Handbags**: Dior's foray into handbags began in the late 1990s, blending the brand's couture sensibilities with practicality. These handbags embodied the elegance and craftsmanship synonymous with the Dior name.
- **Iconic Designs**: The Lady Dior bag, introduced in 1995, became one of the brand's most iconic handbags. Originally named 'Chouchou' (French for 'Favorite'), it was renamed in honor of Princess Diana, who was a fan of the design.

- **Modern Innovations**: Under the creative direction of designers like John Galliano, Raf Simons, and currently Maria Grazia Chiuri, Dior has continued to introduce innovative and stylish handbags. These designs often incorporate the brand's classic motifs while embracing contemporary aesthetics.

Legacy and Cultural Impact

- **Fashion and Artistic Collaborations**: Dior has collaborated with various artists and designers over the years, infusing its collections with artistic influences and maintaining relevance in the ever-evolving world of high fashion.

- **Cultural Icon**: Dior has cemented its status as a cultural icon, with its creations often featured in films, red carpets, and prestigious events, reinforcing its legacy in the fashion industry.

Christian Dior's journey in the world of luxury fashion and handbags is one marked by a commitment to elegance, innovation, and craftsmanship. The brand's strong identity, combined with its ability to continually reinvent and stay relevant, makes it a significant player in the luxury market and a compelling choice for investment. From the iconic New Look to the timeless appeal of the Lady Dior bag, the brand continues to be synonymous with French luxury and global fashion influence.

Hermès: A Legacy of Craftsmanship in Luxury Fashion and Leather Goods

Founding and Early Development

- **Establishment**: Hermès was founded in 1837 by Thierry Hermès as a harness workshop in Paris. Initially, its primary focus was on serving European noblemen, creating high-quality wrought harnesses and bridles for the carriage trade.
- **Expansion to Leather Goods**: Under the leadership of Charles-Émile Hermès, Thierry's son, the company

expanded its offerings to include saddlery and started retail sales. The brand's reputation for quality and craftsmanship began to spread beyond France.

Transition to Luxury Fashion

- **Introduction of Bags**: In the 1920s, Hermès expanded its product line to include accessories, clothing, and handbags. The first handbag was introduced in 1922 when Émile-Maurice's wife complained of not finding a suitable one and he created a line of leather bags for her.
- **The Birth of Iconic Handbags**: The Kelly bag, originally called the Sac à

dépêches, was introduced in the 1930s. It was later renamed after Grace Kelly, the Princess of Monaco, who used it to shield her pregnancy from the paparazzi in 1956.

- **Creation of the Birkin Bag**: The Birkin bag, one of Hermès' most famous handbags, was born from a chance encounter between Jean-Louis Dumas, the then CEO of Hermès, and actress Jane Birkin in 1984. Jane Birkin expressed her difficulty in finding a leather weekend bag she liked, leading to the creation of the now-iconic Birkin bag.

Hermès' Commitment to Quality and Artisanship

- **Artisanal Production**: Hermès is known for its dedication to quality and craftsmanship. Each bag is handcrafted by skilled artisans, a process that can take up to 48 hours per bag.
- **Exclusivity and Demand**: The exclusivity of Hermès products, particularly the Birkin and Kelly bags, is maintained through limited production and high demand, contributing to their status as luxury symbols and investment pieces.

Cultural and Fashion Influence

- **Fashion Innovations**: Beyond handbags, Hermès has been influential in the world of fashion, particularly with its silk scarves, introduced in the 1930s. These scarves have become emblematic of the brand's creativity and luxury status.
- **Brand Expansion**: Today, Hermès remains a family-owned entity, and it has successfully expanded into menswear, perfumery, home goods, and other luxury segments while maintaining its heritage in leather goods and fashion.

Hermès represents the pinnacle of luxury in the fashion world, renowned for its exceptional leather goods, iconic handbags, and silk scarves. The brand's commitment to artisanal craftsmanship, combined with its rich history and timeless designs, has cemented its status as a symbol of elegance and quality. Hermès' handbags, in particular, are not just fashion accessories but also coveted investment pieces, celebrated for their enduring value and appeal.

History of Kering: A Powerhouse in the Luxury Fashion Industry

Founding and Early Years

- **Establishment**: Kering, originally named Pinault S.A., was founded in 1963 by François Pinault. It started as a wood and building materials company, far from the luxury fashion industry it is known for today.
- **Diversification and Expansion**: In the late 1990s, under the leadership of François-Henri Pinault, François's son, the company began a strategic shift

towards the luxury sector. This move marked the beginning of its transformation into a global luxury group.

Transition to Luxury Fashion

- **Acquisition of Luxury Brands**: The pivotal point in Kering's history was the acquisition of the luxury fashion brand Gucci in 1999. This acquisition was a strategic move that placed Kering at the forefront of the luxury fashion world.
- **Further Expansion**: Following the success with Gucci, Kering continued to expand its portfolio, acquiring other high-end brands such as Yves Saint

Laurent, Bottega Veneta, and Balenciaga. Each brand brought its unique style and heritage, enriching Kering's diversity in the luxury market.

Influences and Contributions to Luxury Fashion

- **Gucci's Reinvention**: Under Kering's ownership, Gucci underwent significant changes, particularly with the appointment of Alessandro Michele as Creative Director in 2015. Michele's visionary approach revitalized Gucci, making it a trendsetter in contemporary fashion.
- **Reviving Saint Laurent**: Similarly, Kering's acquisition of Saint Laurent

led to a revival of the brand, especially with Hedi Slimane and later Anthony Vaccarello as creative directors, who injected modernity and relevance into its collections.

- **Innovations in Balenciaga**: Balenciaga, under the creative leadership of designers like Nicolas Ghesquière and Demna Gvasalia, has become known for its innovative and sometimes disruptive fashion statements, further solidifying Kering's reputation for fostering creativity and innovation.

Sustainability and Corporate Responsibility

- **Sustainability Initiatives**: Kering has been a leader in incorporating sustainability into its business model. The group has set ambitious environmental targets, aiming to reduce its carbon footprint and promote ethical and sustainable practices across its brands.

- **Cultural Influence**: Beyond fashion, Kering has played a role in promoting cultural initiatives, supporting art, cinema, and sustainability programs, thereby extending its influence beyond the realms of fashion and luxury.

Kering's transformation from a timber trading company to a titan in the luxury fashion industry is a remarkable story of strategic diversification and visionary leadership. By acquiring and revitalizing some of the world's most prestigious fashion brands, Kering has become a key player in shaping the global luxury fashion landscape. Its commitment to sustainability and corporate responsibility further positions Kering as a forward-thinking leader in the luxury sector, influencing not only fashion trends but also industry standards and practices.

Prada: Innovation and Timelessness in Luxury Fashion

Founding and Early Development

- **Establishment**: Prada was founded in 1913 by Mario Prada in Milan, Italy. Originally named Fratelli Prada, the brand started as a luxury leather goods shop, offering high-quality bags, trunks, and suitcases.
- **Early Recognition**: The brand quickly gained recognition for its sophisticated craftsmanship and was appointed as an official supplier to the Italian royal

family, which helped establish its reputation for luxury.

Transition to Fashion Powerhouse

- **Miuccia Prada's Influence**: The real transformation of Prada began in the late 1970s when Miuccia Prada, Mario's granddaughter, took over the company. Her unique vision and approach to fashion steered Prada into the modern era of luxury.
- **Launch of Nylon Bags**: In 1985, Prada launched its first line of nylon bags, a move that was unconventional at the time. The minimalist design and practicality of these bags were a stark contrast to the prevailing luxury

trends and set a new standard in high-fashion accessories.

Prada's Influence in Fashion

- **Innovative Designs**: Prada is known for its ability to blend high fashion with functional design. The brand has been influential in setting trends, particularly in the 1990s and 2000s, with its avant-garde style.
- **Cultural Impact**: Prada's designs have often reflected and influenced broader cultural and societal trends, making the brand a significant player in the global fashion discourse.

The Collectability of Prada Handbags

- **Iconic Handbags**: Prada's handbags, especially the nylon and saffiano leather collections, have become icons in their own right. The Prada Galleria and the Prada Cahier are examples of handbags that have achieved a status of desirability and collectability.
- **Resale Market and Value**: Prada handbags have held their value well in the resale market, particularly classic styles that embody the brand's minimalist yet luxurious aesthetic.
- **Investment Pieces**: While Prada may not have the same investment cachet as Hermès or Chanel, its handbags are considered a worthwhile investment

for those looking to own a piece of luxury that combines functionality with high fashion.

Prada stands as a testament to the power of innovation and timelessness in the luxury fashion industry. From its early days as a leather goods brand to its status as a fashion innovator, Prada has consistently pushed the boundaries of style and luxury. Its handbags have become emblematic of the brand's ethos, offering a blend of practicality and luxury that resonates with fashion enthusiasts and collectors alike.

Burberry: British Heritage and Iconic Design in Luxury Fashion

Founding and Early Years

- **Establishment**: Burberry was founded in 1856 by Thomas Burberry, a draper's apprentice, who opened his own store in Basingstoke, England. Initially, the brand focused on outdoor attire, especially for the local sportsmen.
- **Innovation of Gabardine**: In 1879, Thomas Burberry invented gabardine, a durable, waterproof, and breathable fabric. This invention revolutionized rainwear and was the foundation of Burberry's early success.

Evolution into a Luxury Fashion Brand

- **Trench Coats and War Influence**: During World War I, Burberry developed the trench coat for military use. After the war, these coats became popular among civilians and were synonymous with the brand's identity.
- **The Burberry Check**: The iconic Burberry check pattern was introduced in the 1920s as a lining to its trench coats. Over time, this pattern emerged as a standalone symbol of the brand, featured on various products and becoming a hallmark of British luxury.

Burberry in Modern Fashion

- **Expansion and Diversification**: Throughout the 20th century, Burberry expanded its range to include more ready-to-wear fashion, accessories, and fragrances, while maintaining its reputation for quality and British heritage.
- **Revitalization Efforts**: In the late 1990s and early 2000s, Burberry underwent a transformation under the leadership of CEO Rose Marie Bravo and later, creative director Christopher Bailey. They modernized the brand while respecting its heritage, broadening its appeal.

Collectability of Burberry Products

- **The Appeal of the Trench Coat**: Burberry's trench coats have remained highly collectible items, prized for their craftsmanship and timeless design. Vintage Burberry trench coats, especially those with the classic check lining, are sought after by collectors and fashion enthusiasts.
- **Iconic Accessories**: Burberry's scarves, handbags, and other accessories featuring the Burberry check have become symbols of luxury and are popular in the collectibles market.
- **Investment Potential**: While Burberry might not command the same resale value as brands like Chanel or Hermès, its products are considered a solid

investment for those seeking classic style and enduring quality.

Conclusion

Burberry's journey from a humble outdoor attire shop to a symbol of British luxury fashion is marked by innovation, a commitment to quality, and a keen understanding of its heritage. The brand's iconic trench coats, distinctive check pattern, and modern yet timeless designs have cemented its status as a key player in the luxury fashion industry. Burberry's products, revered for their craftsmanship and style, continue to be valued by collectors and fashion lovers around the world.

Chapter 4

Evaluating Investment-Worthy Handbags

In the vibrant world of luxury handbags, the allure of aesthetic beauty is often equally matched by the prospect of financial appreciation. This chapter delves into the art of discerning which handbags stand as mere emblems of fashion and which transcend to become worthy investments.

The Essence of a Brand's Legacy
When it comes to investment potential, the story behind a brand is as crucial as the handbag itself. Luxury brands like Hermès, Chanel, and Louis Vuitton aren't just selling a product; they're offering a piece of history, a

slice of artisanship. The Birkin, for instance, is not merely a bag; it's a narrative of exclusivity and luxury. Similarly, Chanel's Flap Bag isn't just a fashion statement; it's a timeless classic that carries Coco Chanel's legacy of elegance. In assessing a handbag's worth as an investment, one must weigh the brand's history, its position in the luxury market, and its track record in sustaining and growing the value of its products.

Rarity: The Key to Value

Limited editions and exclusive releases are often synonymous with higher investment potential. A handbag's rarity can significantly enhance its desirability among collectors and enthusiasts. For instance, a limited-edition

Hermès Birkin with unique features or a Chanel handbag from a rare collaboration can fetch significantly higher prices in the secondary market than their standard counterparts. The principle is simple: the harder a bag is to acquire, the more valuable it becomes.

Timelessness Over Trends

While the allure of trendy handbags is undeniable, their investment potential can be fleeting. In contrast, handbags boasting timeless designs promise enduring appeal, making them safer and often more lucrative investment options. A classic Louis Vuitton Speedy, for instance, has retained its charm and resale value for decades, outliving countless fashion trends. Investment-worthy handbags often embody classic aesthetics, versatile functionality, and enduring brand value.

Craftsmanship and Quality: A Closer Look

The materials and craftsmanship that go into creating a luxury handbag directly impact its longevity and future value. High-quality leather that ages well, exotic skins, sturdy hardware that resists wear and tear, and meticulous stitching are all hallmarks of a well-crafted handbag. Moreover, the expertise and time invested in handcrafting these pieces add to their exclusivity and, consequently, their investment potential.

Condition and Authenticity: Non-Negotiables

The condition of a handbag is paramount in determining its investment value. A well-preserved handbag, preferably with minimal signs of wear and its original packaging, will always command a higher price.

Authenticity is equally critical. Investing in a luxury handbag entails ensuring its genuineness, which can be verified through brand-specific characteristics, expert authentication services, or direct verification from the brand itself.

Navigating Market Trends

An astute investor in luxury handbags must keep a finger on the pulse of the market. This involves not only tracking current trends but also anticipating future collectibles. Understanding consumer behavior, staying attuned to the fashion world's shifts, and recognizing emerging classics before they soar in popularity are skills that can significantly enhance investment success.

Strategic Acquisition: Buying Smart

Investing in luxury handbags isn't just about what to buy; it's also about when and where. Purchasing a handbag at retail price might be worthwhile for newly released models with high demand, while the secondary market could offer better deals for vintage or rare pieces. Timing, they say, is everything. Buying a handbag before it becomes widely popular or acquiring a vintage piece just as it re-enters the fashion zeitgeist can result in a savvy investment.

Investing in luxury handbags merges the worlds of fashion enthusiasm and financial strategy. It requires a blend of passion, knowledge, and foresight. Whether it's a classic Chanel that speaks of timeless elegance or a rare Hermès that stands as a testament to unparalleled luxury, the key to successful handbag investment lies in understanding and appreciating the nuances that make these items more than just accessories, but valuable assets in the world of fashion and beyond.

Chapter 5

Authenticity and Quality in Luxury Handbags

In the realm of luxury handbags, authenticity and quality are paramount. With the rise of 'super fakes' in the market, discerning the genuine from the counterfeit is more crucial than ever. This chapter provides an in-depth look into the importance of authenticity verification, spotting counterfeits, and understanding the quality markers of top luxury brands.

The Importance of Authenticity Verification
The essence of a luxury handbag's value lies in its authenticity. Authentic pieces are testaments to the brand's legacy,

craftsmanship, and their potential as investment pieces.

- **Brand Heritage and Craftsmanship**: True luxury handbags from brands like Hermès and Chanel carry a heritage of artisanship. The quality of materials and craftsmanship in authentic bags can't be replicated in counterfeits.
- **Value and Resale**: Genuine luxury handbags hold significant resale value, often appreciating over time, unlike counterfeit items that hold no value in the luxury resale market.
- **Consumer Confidence**: Authenticity verification ensures consumer trust in

the brand and the luxury market, safeguarding the buyer's investment.

Spotting Counterfeits and Understanding Quality Markers

Recognizing counterfeit luxury handbags requires an understanding of the subtle details that distinguish genuine pieces from fakes.

- **Material Quality**: Authentic luxury handbags are crafted from high-grade materials — the leather, metal, and fabric have a quality feel, distinct smell, and visual appeal that counterfeits often fail to replicate.

-

- **Craftsmanship and Details**: Genuine luxury bags have impeccable craftsmanship. For example, Hermès bags are known for their even, slant-free stitching and perfectly aligned patterns.
- **Brand-specific Features**: Familiarity with brand-specific features is crucial in spotting fakes. Chanel bags have a specific quilt size and pattern, and authentic Louis Vuitton pieces showcase symmetrical and clear monogram prints.

Hallmarks of Authenticity in Top Brands

Hermès

- **Precision in Craftsmanship**: Authentic Hermès handbags, like the Birkin and Kelly, are hand-sewn with meticulous attention to detail, making their stitching a key indicator of authenticity. The measurements of the bag's dimensions are perfection. A 35cm is precisely 35cm – not one millimeter more or less.
- **Hardware and Locks**: Each Hermès bag features high-quality hardware with unique lock numbers, a feature often overlooked in counterfeits. There are lists online of the serial numbers of fake Hermes locks. The

pochette that holds the keys is made from a single, folded piece of leather.
- **Inside Zipper:** Hermes inside zippers feature a custom-made H-zipper with a leather pull that lays horizontally without droop.

Chanel
- **Quilting and Stitching**: Chanel's iconic quilts are symmetrical with a consistent pattern – each square is 3cm x 3cm.. The stitching is precise, and the lining fits perfectly, ensuring no bulges or misalignments.
- **Serial Stickers and Cards**: Chanel bags come with serial number stickers and

authenticity cards that match, a feature often misrepresented in counterfeit items. Check the authenticity card carefully for spelling errors.

Louis Vuitton

- **Monogram Canvas**: The monogram pattern on authentic Louis Vuitton bags is crisp, clear, and symmetrically aligned, a detail often fumbled by counterfeiters.
- **Stitching Consistency**: Louis Vuitton uses a specific yellow thread for stitching, with an even and regular

pattern, distinguishing it from the often irregular stitching of fakes.

Resources and Expert Opinions for Authentication

Leveraging expert resources is essential for accurate authentication.

- **Professional Authentication Services**: Entrupy, Authenticate First, and Real Authentication offer reliable services for verifying the authenticity of luxury handbags.
- **Brand Verification**: Visiting an official store for verification is a reliable method, as many luxury brands offer in-house authentication services.

- **Online Forums and Communities**: Platforms like The Purse Forum provide a community-driven approach to authentication, offering insights and advice from fellow enthusiasts and experts.

Navigating the luxury handbag market with an understanding of authenticity and quality is vital. Recognizing the craftsmanship of genuine pieces, being aware of the hallmarks of top brands, and staying informed about the prevalence of super fakes are key to making informed decisions. This knowledge not only protects the investment but also upholds the integrity and legacy of the luxury handbags.

Chapter 6

Buying and Selling Designer Handbags

Chapter 6

Buying and Selling

Designer Handbags

The art of buying and selling designer handbags involves navigating through various markets and platforms, each with its own nuances. This chapter provides detailed insights into the primary and secondary luxury handbag markets, offers practical tips for buying, and outlines effective strategies for selling handbags to maximize investment returns.

Navigating the Primary and Secondary Luxury Handbag Markets

Primary Market: Boutiques and Official Retailers

- **Exclusivity and Latest Collections**: The primary market offers the latest collections directly from the brands. Purchasing from official boutiques or retailers ensures authenticity and access to exclusive pieces.
- **Relationship Building**: Buying from the primary market allows for building relationships with brand representatives, which can be beneficial for future purchases, especially for limited-edition or high-demand items.

Secondary Market: Pre-owned Luxury

- **Diverse Selection**: The secondary market offers a wide range of pre-owned handbags, including vintage and rare finds. Platforms like The RealReal, Vestiaire Collective, and Fashionphile are popular for their vast selections.

- **Authenticity and Condition**: Key considerations in the secondary market include the authenticity and condition of the handbags. Buyers should meticulously verify authenticity and assess the condition of the item, as it significantly impacts value.

Tips for Buying: Auctions, Boutiques, and Online Platforms

Auctions

- **Rare and Vintage Finds**: Auctions are ideal for finding rare, vintage, and collector handbags. Houses like Christie's and Sotheby's regularly feature luxury handbag auctions.
- **Research and Due Diligence**: Before participating in an auction, research the item's provenance, condition reports, and market value. Understanding the auction house's terms and fees is also crucial.

Boutiques

- **Personalized Experience**: Buying from brand boutiques offers a personalized shopping experience. Customers can inspect the handbags firsthand and receive expert advice from brand representatives.
- **Brand Guarantees**: Purchases from official boutiques come with brand guarantees, authenticity certificates, and often a favorable return policy.

Online Platforms

- **Convenience and Variety**: Online platforms provide the convenience of browsing a wide range of handbags from different brands in one place.

- **Vetting Sellers and Platforms**: It's important to vet sellers and platforms for their credibility, return policies, and customer reviews. Authenticity verification services provided by the platform should be scrutinized.

Strategies for Selling and Maximizing Investment Returns

Timing the Market

- **Understanding Market Trends**: Successful selling involves understanding current fashion trends and market demand. Timing the sale when the demand for a particular style or brand is high can significantly increase the sale price.

- **Seasonal Considerations**: Seasonal trends can also influence the sale price. For instance, selling a beach tote in summer might yield better returns than in winter.

Choosing the Right Platform

- **Selecting the Platform Based on the Handbag Type**: Choose a selling platform that aligns with the handbag's brand, model, and target audience. For high-value, rare, or vintage handbags, auction houses or high-end consignment platforms may be more suitable.

- **Online Marketplaces**: Platforms like eBay, The RealReal, and Vestiaire Collective cater to a wide audience and offer various tools and services to facilitate the selling process.

Presentation and Authenticity

- **Quality Presentation**: Good quality photographs and detailed descriptions can increase the handbag's appeal. Include images of unique features, authenticity certificates, and any signs of wear.
- **Providing Proof of Authenticity**: Including proof of authenticity and purchase enhances buyer trust. For handbags bought on the secondary

market, having them authenticated by a reputable service can add value.

Buying and selling designer handbags requires strategic thinking, thorough market research, and an understanding of the dynamics of different sales platforms. By carefully navigating the primary and secondary markets, leveraging the right platforms, and timing sales strategically, enthusiasts and investors can optimize their experiences and maximize returns on their luxury handbag investments.

Chapter 7

Risks and Rewards of Handbag Investing

Investing in designer handbags is an enticing venture for many, blending the allure of fashion with the potential for financial gain. However, like any investment, it comes with its own set of risks and rewards. This chapter delves deeply into the dynamics of handbag investing, highlighting the potential risks, strategies for portfolio diversification, and drawing lessons from both success stories and common pitfalls.

Analyzing the Risks Involved in Handbag Investment

Market Volatility

- **Fashion Trends**: The luxury handbag market is susceptible to changing fashion trends. A style or brand that is highly sought-after today might not retain the same demand in the future.

- **Economic Fluctuations**: Global economic downturns can impact luxury spending, affecting the resale value and demand for high-end handbags.

Authenticity Concerns

- **Counterfeits and Super Fakes**: The market is rife with counterfeits, including high-quality replicas that can be difficult to distinguish from genuine

- articles, posing significant risks to uninformed investors.

Condition and Maintenance
- **Degradation Over Time**: Handbags, being physical assets, can degrade over time if not properly cared for, impacting their value significantly.
- **Storage and Upkeep**: Proper storage and maintenance are essential to preserve a handbag's condition, which requires ongoing effort and sometimes additional investment.

Balancing Portfolio with Handbags as Alternative Investments

Diversification Benefits

- **Non-Correlation with Traditional Assets**: Handbags often have a low correlation with traditional investment assets like stocks and bonds, making them a good diversification tool.
- **Hedge Against Inflation**: In some cases, luxury handbags have outperformed traditional investments, acting as a hedge against inflation.

Allocation Strategy

- **Percentage of Portfolio**: It's prudent for investors to allocate only a portion of their investment portfolio to luxury handbags, ensuring a balanced approach to risk.

- **Brand and Style Diversification**: Investing in a diverse range of brands and styles can mitigate risk. While some brands have a strong track record, emerging designers or limited editions might offer surprising returns.

Pitfalls to Avoid

Common Pitfalls

- **Overpaying in Secondary Market**: Caution against overpaying for handbags in the secondary market without proper valuation knowledge, which can lead to losses.

- **Neglecting Research**: Emphasize the risks of investing without adequate research into market trends, brand value, and authenticity verification.
- **Emotional Decisions Over Rational Investing**: Warn against letting personal taste override investment rationale, as not all aesthetically pleasing handbags are good investments.

Investing in designer handbags can be a rewarding endeavor, offering both financial gains and the pleasure of owning beautiful fashion pieces. However, it requires careful consideration, informed decision-making, and an understanding of the market's intricacies. By acknowledging the risks, strategically diversifying investment portfolios, and learning from both triumphs and missteps in the market, investors can navigate this unique field with greater confidence and success.

Chapter 8

Care and Maintenance of Investment Handbags

Investing in luxury handbags isn't just about the initial purchase; it's also about maintaining their beauty and value over time. Proper care, storage, and maintenance are crucial for preserving the condition and thus the investment potential of your luxury handbags. Let's explore the best practices and considerations to ensure your prized possessions withstand the test of time.

Best Practices for Storage, Care, and Maintenance

Proper Storage

- **Avoid Direct Sunlight and Humidity**: Store your handbags in a cool, dry place away from direct sunlight to prevent fading and leather damage.
- **Appropriate Spacing**: Ensure your handbags are not cramped or pressed against hard surfaces, as this can cause deformation and creasing.
- **Dust Bags and Stuffing**: Use soft, breathable dust bags for storage. Stuffing your handbags with acid-free tissue paper helps maintain their shape.

Regular Care

- **Routine Cleaning**: Regularly wipe down your handbags with a soft, dry cloth to remove surface dust. For leather bags, use specific leather cleaners and conditioners to keep the material supple.
- **Handling with Clean Hands**: Always handle your bags with clean hands or white cotton gloves to avoid transferring oils and dirt.
- **Avoid Overloading**: Don't overstuff your handbags, as excessive weight can strain and stretch the handles and leather.

Long-term Maintenance

- **Climate Control**: If possible, store your handbags in a climate-controlled environment to prevent damage from extreme temperatures.
- **Rotating Usage**: Regularly rotate the use of your handbags to prevent excessive wear and tear on any single item.

The Impact of Condition on Value

Maintaining Pristine Condition

- **Value Retention**: The closer a handbag is to its original condition, the higher its value in the resale market. Signs of wear, tear, or damage can significantly decrease its value.

- **Documentation of Care**: Keeping a record of maintenance and care, including professional cleaning or repairs, can add value by demonstrating responsible ownership.

Signs of Wear

- **Surface Scratches and Stains**: Minor scratches and stains can be seen as normal wear, but significant damage or discoloration can drastically reduce a bag's value.
- **Interior Condition**: The interior condition is as important as the exterior. Stains, pen marks, or tears inside the bag can detract from its overall value.

Restoration and Repair Considerations

When to Consider Professional Restoration

- **Assessing the Damage**: For high-value handbags, professional restoration can be a wise investment. Assess the extent of wear or damage to determine if professional services are warranted.
- **Choosing the Right Service**: opt for restoration services specializing in luxury handbags. Some brands offer their own repair services, which is usually the best option for high-end bags.

Risks of Restoration

- **Potential Value Loss**: In some cases, restoration, especially if not done professionally, can reduce a handbag's value, particularly for vintage pieces where originality is key.
- **Restoration vs. Preservation**: Sometimes, it's better to preserve a bag in its current state rather than risk improper restoration. This is especially true for vintage handbags where patina and original features are valued.

The care and maintenance of luxury handbags are as essential as their initial purchase. By adhering to best practices in storage, routine care, and considering professional restoration judiciously, you can ensure that your handbags not only retain their beauty and functionality but also their value as investment pieces. Remember, the way you care for your luxury handbag can significantly influence its longevity and resale value, making maintenance an integral part of your investment strategy.

Chapter 9

The Future of Handbag Investing

The landscape of handbag investing is continually evolving, shaped by various factors that range from changing consumer preferences to technological innovations. As an investor in luxury handbags, it's crucial to stay ahead of these trends to make informed decisions. This chapter explores the emerging trends, the growing emphasis on sustainability, and the impact of technological advancements on the luxury handbag market.

Emerging Trends and Future Predictions

The Shift Towards Unique and Artisanal Pieces

- **Demand for Uniqueness**: There is an increasing trend toward unique, artisanal handbags that offer a sense of individuality and exclusivity. Handcrafted pieces from smaller, niche designers are gaining popularity among collectors and investors.
- **Limited Editions and Collaborations**: Collaborations between luxury brands and artists or other brands are creating highly sought-after limited-edition pieces, which are often seen as good investment opportunities due to their uniqueness and limited availability.

The Resurgence of Vintage Styles

- **Vintage Revival**: The allure of vintage and retro styles continues to grow. There is a strong market for older, classic models from top brands, as these pieces often have historical significance and a story that resonates with collectors.

The Influence of Digital Platforms and Social Media

- **Online Market Influence**: The rise of digital platforms and social media is significantly influencing consumer preferences and trends. The visibility and hype generated on these platforms can quickly elevate a handbag's status and demand.

The Role of Sustainability and Ethical Considerations

Growing Consumer Consciousness

- **Sustainability**: There's a growing awareness and demand for sustainability in fashion. Luxury brands are increasingly adopting eco-friendly materials and ethical manufacturing processes.
- **Ethical Sourcing and Production**: Consumers are more informed and concerned about how their luxury handbags are sourced and produced.

Brands that prioritize ethical practices are likely to be favored in future investment decisions.

The Impact on Investment

- **Long-Term Value**: Sustainable and ethically produced handbags are poised to hold long-term value as consumer preferences shift towards environmentally and socially responsible products.
- **Brand Reputation**: Brands that proactively adopt sustainable practices are likely to enhance their reputation and desirability, impacting the future value of their handbags.

Technological Advancements and Their Impact

Innovation in Materials and Manufacturing

- **Advanced Materials**: The development of new, high-quality sustainable materials is set to revolutionize the handbag industry. These materials may offer new aesthetics and functionalities, appealing to a broader market.
- **Production Efficiency**: Technological advancements in manufacturing can lead to more efficient production processes, potentially lowering costs and reducing environmental impact.

Authentication and Blockchain Technology

- **Fighting Counterfeits**: Advances in technology are playing a crucial role in the authentication of luxury handbags. Blockchain technology, for instance, provides a secure and unchangeable record of a handbag's history, authenticity, and ownership.
- **Digital Provenance**: The use of digital tracking and provenance tools offers transparency and security in handbag investing, ensuring the authenticity and history of investment pieces are easily verifiable.

The future of handbag investing is vibrant and dynamic, influenced by a blend of traditional luxury values and modern considerations like sustainability and technology. As an investor, staying informed about these trends and adapting your strategy accordingly can lead to more informed and potentially lucrative investment decisions. Embracing change, being mindful of emerging consumer preferences, and leveraging technology will be key to navigating the future landscape of luxury handbag investing.

Conclusion

MASTERING THE ART OF

LUXURY

HANDBAG INVESTMENT

As we conclude our exploration into the captivating world of luxury handbag investment, it's evident that this venture combines an appreciation for fashion and art with savvy financial acumen. The journey through the histories, iconic models, and investment strategies of the world's most esteemed luxury brands illuminates a path not only to owning exquisite pieces of craftsmanship but also to embracing a form of investment that is both tangible and emotionally rewarding.

Summarizing Key Strategies

- **Research and Knowledge**: An informed investor is a successful one. Understanding the history, craftsmanship, and market demand of luxury handbags is paramount.
- **Authenticity and Quality**: The cornerstone of handbag investment. Always ensure authenticity and maintain the quality of your handbags, as these factors significantly impact their value.
- **Market Trends and Timing**: Stay attuned to fashion trends and market shifts. The right timing for buying and selling can substantially affect investment returns.

- **Diversification**: Just like any investment portfolio, diversification within your handbag collection can mitigate risk. Include a mix of classic staples and potential future classics from different brands.
- **Long-Term Perspective**: Luxury handbag investment often requires a long-term view, appreciating the gradual increase in value and the joy of collecting.

The Evolving Landscape of Luxury Handbags
The landscape of luxury handbags is ever-evolving, shaped by cultural shifts, fashion trends, and technological advancements. Sustainability and ethical production are

becoming increasingly significant, influencing brand strategies and consumer preferences. The digital era has transformed the way we buy, sell, and interact with luxury brands, making the market more accessible and dynamic.

Despite these changes, the core allure of luxury handbags remains steadfast - a blend of aesthetic beauty, craftsmanship, and the prestige of owning a piece of a storied brand. As new designs emerge and vintage pieces resurface with renewed interest, the market for luxury handbags continues to offer diverse opportunities for both seasoned collectors and new investors.

Final Thoughts...

Investing in luxury handbags is more than just acquiring beautiful objects; it's about participating in a legacy of fashion and luxury. It's a journey that rewards patience, passion, and discernment. Whether you're drawn to the timeless elegance of a Chanel Classic Flap Bag, the bold statement of a Gucci Dionysus, or the understated sophistication of a Celine Luggage Tote, each handbag you choose to invest in is a testament to your personal story within the vast tapestry of luxury fashion.

As you close this book, may you carry forward the insights and strategies shared, ready to navigate the vibrant and rewarding world of luxury handbag investment with confidence and style.

Appendix A

GLOSSARY OF TERMS

- **Authentication**: Verification process to confirm a handbag's authenticity, often involving expert examination of materials, craftsmanship, logos, and serial numbers.
- **Collector's Item**: A handbag that is highly sought after by collectors for its rarity, design, historical significance, or association with specific events or personalities.
- **Condition Grades**: A system to categorize the condition of pre-owned handbags, typically ranging from 'Mint' (like new) to 'Fair' (shows significant signs of wear).

- **Consignment**: The process of selling a handbag through a third party who takes a portion of the sale price as a fee.
- **Counterfeit**: A fake or imitation handbag designed to look like it is from a high-end brand, often made using inferior materials and craftsmanship.
- **Heritage Brand**: A luxury brand that has a long history and established reputation in the fashion industry.
- **Investment Bag**: A designer handbag purchased with the intention of it holding or increasing in value over time.

- **Limited Edition**: A handbag produced in restricted quantities, often featuring unique designs, colors, or collaborations, enhancing its rarity and potential investment value.
- **Provenance**: The history of a handbag, including its origins, previous ownership, and any significant events associated with it, which can influence its value.
- **Resale Value**: The potential price a handbag can fetch in the secondary market. Factors influencing this include brand, condition, rarity, and demand.
- **Serial Number**: A unique code assigned to a luxury handbag, often

used for identification and authentication purposes.

- **Vintage**: In the context of handbags, refers to items that are at least 20 years old. Vintage pieces often have additional value due to their historical significance.

Appendix B

ENHANCED DIRECTORY OF RESOURCES FOR AUTHENTICATION, BUYING, AND SELLING

Authentication Services

- **Entrupy**: Utilizes AI and machine learning technology to offer a high-tech solution for authenticating luxury handbags, boasting a high accuracy rate.
    - Website: Entrupy
- **Authenticate First**: Provides detailed authentication services for a variety of luxury brands, offering peace of mind to buyers and sellers.
    - Website: Authenticate First
- **Real Authentication**: Known for a team of industry experts, this service offers authentication services for a wide range of luxury handbag brands.

- Website: Real Authentication
- **Retailer Authentication**: Many luxury brands offer authentication services through their official retail stores. Visiting a brand's flagship store or an authorized retailer can be a reliable way to authenticate a handbag.

Online Marketplaces for Buying and Selling

- **The RealReal**: Offers a large selection of authenticated pre-owned luxury handbags, with a thorough authentication process conducted by experts.
  - Website: The RealReal

- **Vestiaire Collective**: A globally recognized platform for pre-owned luxury and designer fashion, where each item is checked by expert authenticators before sale.
  - Website: Vestiaire Collective
- **Fashionphile**: Specializes in buying and selling pre-owned luxury handbags, providing detailed condition reports and a unique buy-back program.
  - Website: Fashionphile

There are many, many online marketplaces for luxury handbags, with more appearing every day. Pay close attention to the grammar and spelling. One way fraudsters identify a "mark" is to rule out people who pay attention to detail. Be someone who is attuned to detail. Reviews can be faked. Return policies can be faked. Don't overlook the small details.

Auction Houses Specializing in Luxury Goods

- **Sotheby's**: A prestigious auction house hosting sales for rare and valuable luxury handbags, known for featuring collector's items and limited editions.
    - Website: Sotheby's
- **Christie's**: Conducts auctions for high-end handbags, offering a range of rare and collectible luxury items with expert valuation and authentication.

- Website: Christie's
- **Heritage Auctions**: Offers a variety of luxury auctions, including ones specifically for designer handbags, with a wide selection of brands and rare pieces.
    - Website: Heritage Auctions

Appendix C

REFERENCE LIST OF KEY HANDBAG MODELS FROM TOP BRANDS

Hermès

- **Birkin Bag**: An iconic bag known for its investment value, often appreciating over time.
- **Kelly Bag**: Another classic Hermès style, famous for its elegant design and association with Grace Kelly.
- **Constance Bag**: A less common but highly coveted design with a signature 'H' clasp.

Chanel

- **Classic Flap Bag**: Known for its quilted leather and CC clasp, a staple in luxury investment.

- **2.55 Reissue Bag**: The original design by Coco Chanel, known for its historical significance and classic style.
- **Boy Bag**: Introduced in 2011, this bag has quickly become a modern classic with investment potential.

Louis Vuitton

- **Neverfull Tote**: A popular tote known for its durability and resale value.
- **Speedy Bag**: A classic design, known for its versatility and status as a collector's item.
- **Alma Bag**: Recognized for its unique shape and has been a staple in the LV collection for decades.

Gucci

- **Dionysus Bag**: Known for its unique closure and strong resale value.
- **Soho Disco Bag**: A popular crossbody bag, valued for its design and functionality.
- **Marmont Bag**: Features the GG logo and is known for its quilted leather.

Prada

- **Galleria Bag**: A timeless design, often retaining a significant proportion of its retail price on the resale market.
- **Saffiano Lux Tote**: Known for its durable Saffiano leather and elegant design.

- **Nylon Backpack**: Marked a shift in luxury bag materials and remains popular for its versatility and durable design.

Fendi

- **Baguette Bag**: A revolutionary design known for its compact size and association with Carrie Bradshaw in "Sex and the City."
- **Peekaboo Bag**: Known for its unique construction, which allows the interior to peek out from the exterior.
- **Kan I Bag**: Features the iconic Fendi logo and is celebrated for its contemporary and versatile design.

Valentino

- **Rockstud Spike Bag**: Famous for its pyramid studs, blending edginess with elegance.
- **VLogo Signature Bag**: Showcases the bold VLogo and is known for its sophisticated silhouette.
- **Roman Stud Bag**: A newer design featuring oversized studs, combining traditional craftsmanship with modern flair.

Christian Dior

- **Lady Dior Bag**: Known for its quilted texture and 'D.I.O.R' charms, a symbol of elegance and refinement.

- **Saddle Bag**: A unique, equestrian-inspired design that gained cult status in the fashion world.
- **Book Tote**: A recent addition known for its practicality and stylish canvas design, often adorned with intricate embroidery.

Saint Laurent

- **Loulou Bag**: Named after Yves Saint Laurent's muse Loulou de la Falaise, known for its quilted design and YSL monogram.
- **Sac de Jour Bag**: A structured tote that offers a sophisticated and timeless appeal.

- **Kate Bag**: Recognizable for its sleek design and prominent YSL logo, a popular choice for evening wear.

Celine

- **Luggage Tote**: Known for its unique 'face-like' design and spacious interior, a favorite among fashion insiders.
- **Classic Box Bag**: A minimalistic and timeless shoulder bag that exudes understated luxury.
- **Trio Bag**: Popular for its simplicity and functionality, featuring three separate pouches in a compact design.